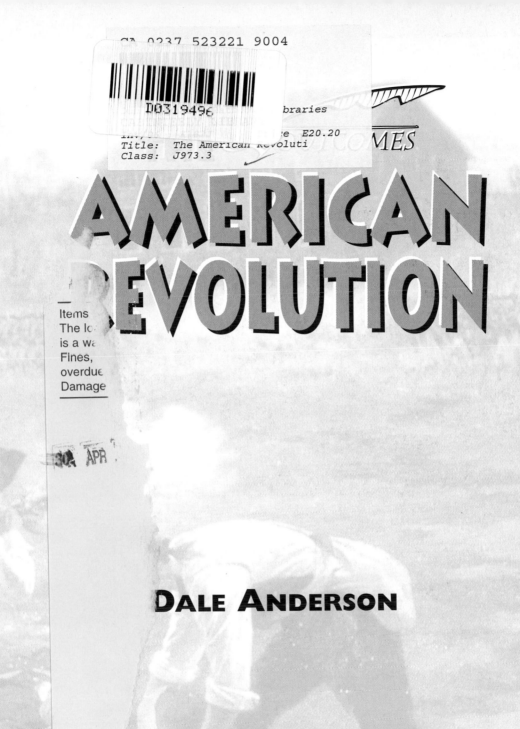

AMERICAN REVOLUTION

DALE ANDERSON

Evans

Evans Brothers Limited

Published by Evans Brothers Limited
2A Portman Mansions
Chiltern Street
London W1U 6NR
UK

First published in 2002

British Library Cataloguing in Publication Data
Anderson, Dale
  The American Revolution. - (Events and outcomes)
  1.United States - History - Revolution, 1775-1783
    Juvenile literature
  I.Title
  973.3

ISBN 0237523221

Edited by Rachel Norridge
Designed by Neil Sayer
Maps by Tim Smith
Consultant: Dr John Kirk

Acknowledgements

Cover Peter Newark's American Pictures **Background image** Peter Newark's American Pictures **p.6** Peter Newark's American Pictures **p.7** (top) Bridgeman Art Library (bottom) Peter Newark's American Pictures **p.8** Peter Newark's American Pictures **p.9** Bridgeman Art Library **p.10** Peter Newark's American Pictures **p.12** Mary Evans Picture Library **p.13** (top) Bridgeman Art Library (bottom) Peter Newark's American Pictures **p.14** Peter Newark's American Pictures **p.15** Peter Newark's American Pictures **p.16** Peter Newark's American Pictures **p.17** (top) Peter Newark's American Pictures (bottom) Peter Newark's American Pictures **p.18** Peter Newark's American Pictures **p.19** Bridgeman Art Library **p.20** (top) Mary Evans Picture Library (bottom) Peter Newark's American Pictures **p.21** Peter Newark's American Pictures **p.22** Peter Newark's American Pictures **p.23** Peter Newark's American Pictures **p.24** Peter Newark's American Pictures **p.25** (top) Bridgeman Art Library (bottom) Peter Newark's American Pictures **p.27** (middle) Peter Newark's American Pictures (bottom) Bridgeman Art Library **p.28** Peter Newark's American Pictures **p.29** Bridgeman Art Library **p.30** Peter Newark's American Pictures **p.31** Mary Evans Picture Library **p.32** Peter Newark's American Pictures **p.33** Peter Newark's American Pictures **p.34** (top) Peter Newark's American Pictures (bottom) Mary Evans Picture Library **p.36** (top) Peter Newark's American Pictures (bottom) Bridgeman Art Library **p.37** Peter Newark's American Pictures **p.38** Bridgeman Art Library **p.40** Peter Newark's American Pictures **p.41** Bridgeman Art Library **p.43** Bridgeman Art Library **p.44** Peter Newark's American Pictures **p.45** Peter Newark's American Pictures **p.46** Corbis **p.47** (top) Mary Evans Picture Library (bottom) Peter Newark's American Pictures **p.48** Peter Newark's American Pictures **p.49** Peter Newark's American Pictures **p.50** Mary Evans Picture Library **p.52** Peter Newark's American Pictures **p.53** Peter Newark's American Pictures **p.54** Corbis **p.55** Peter Newark's American Pictures **p.57** Corbis **p.58** Corbis **p.59** Peter Newark's American Pictures **p.60** Mary Evans Picture Library **p.61** Peter Newark's American Pictures **p.62** Peter Newark's American Pictures **p.63** (top) Peter Newark's American Pictures (bottom) Corbis **p.64** Peter Newark's American Pictures **p.65** (top) Peter Newark's American Pictures (bottom) Corbis **p.66** Bridgeman Art Library **p.67** (top) Peter Newark's American Pictures (bottom) Topham Picturepoint **p.68** Topham Picturepoint **p.69** Bridgeman Art Library **p.70** Peter Newark's American Pictures **p.71** Peter Newark's American Pictures **p.72** Bridgeman Art Library

CONTENTS

WHY A REVOLUTION?

In 1776, the British colonists of North America declared independence. This act came in the early stages of the American Revolution. Yet not that long before, American colonists had been contented, if critical, members of the British Empire. Benjamin Franklin, a noted colonial leader, described how the American colonists saw themselves and Britain:

They had not only a respect, but an affection, for Great Britain, for its laws, its customs and manners, and even a fondness for its fashions.

What had happened? What had made such warm relations turn to war? To understand the causes and course of the American Revolution, we must look at the colonies before the Revolution began.

The Thirteen Colonies

The thirteen American colonies stretched from New Hampshire to Georgia. They could be divided into three regional groups. The New England colonies of the North included New Hampshire, Massachusetts, Connecticut and Rhode Island. Most of the inhabitants were farmers, but the land was generally poor.

Farming was the chief occupation in the American colonies. Subsistence farming was the rule in New England. The middle colonies grew crops for export, and the Southern colonies produced cotton and tobacco on plantations.

An eighteenth-century view of Boston.

As a result, farms were small and produced little surplus. Shipbuilding, fishing and trade were important sources of livelihood. Massachusetts was one of the most populous colonies. Boston, its chief city, was an important centre of business and ideas.

The middle colonies – New York, New Jersey, Pennsylvania and Delaware – had thriving economies. They grew wheat for export and carried on trade. Philadelphia, in Pennsylvania, was the largest city in all the colonies and a major port.

The five Southern colonies were Maryland, Virginia, North and South Carolina and Georgia. They grew tobacco, rice and indigo on large plantations. Large landowners, called planters, relied on slave labour to carry out this work. The planters dominated society and politics.

The Colonists

African American slaves – about 40 per cent of the people in the South – worked on tobacco and other plantations.

Most colonists were of British descent. There were pockets of people from other lands, such as former Dutch settlers in New York and German newcomers in Pennsylvania. In addition, of course, there were large numbers of Africans, especially in the South. The vast majority of these Africans were slaves with no rights.

Governing the Colonies

From the start, the British government had little control over the colonies. Royal charters that created the colonies gave individuals or groups a fair amount of freedom of action within them. In addition, Britain was preoccupied by internal struggles for much of the 1600s.

In the late seventeenth century, the Crown took greater control in the colonies. Charters were revoked, and almost all the colonies became royal colonies. As a result, the monarch appointed a royal governor, who served as the colony's executive.

Despite this, each colony continued to enjoy a large degree of self-government. Voters elected representatives for the legislatures that served in each colony. These assemblies made laws and enacted taxes. As a result, they had some power over the royal governors, who depended on the tax revenues.

The colonists objected strongly when the Crown or royal governors tried to assert their power. The 1600s saw rebellions in Virginia, Massachusetts, New York and Pennsylvania. Each time, colonists were protesting at the power of central authority.

This political cartoon depicts an election day in Philadelphia in the 1760s. The American colonists debated political issues intensely.

The Importance of Trade

To the British, the colonies were a source of economic power. According to the theory called mercantilism, a nation hoped to increase its wealth through trade. When it exported manufactured goods to other countries, it received gold and silver in payment. If it exported more than it imported, its store of gold and silver would grow. Colonies were supposed to supply the raw materials needed to make manufactured goods. Colonists were also expected to buy those goods.

Trade, then, tied colonies to the mother country. Parliament, the legislature in Britain, passed laws to control trade. For instance, the colonies had to ship their products to Britain or other British colonies. Trade with other countries or their colonies was illegal. Duties, or taxes on imports, were placed on some goods to make the sale of British goods more profitable.

By the middle 1700s, these laws had been on the books for decades but were overlooked. Britain followed a policy called 'salutary neglect', that is, the laws were not enforced. Colonial merchants were known to smuggle, or bring in goods illegally. The British simply looked the other way.

The colonies grew and prospered. They revelled in being part of the British Empire. Equally important, they enjoyed being left alone. There was just one worry – the threat of French power in North America. But soon that threat would be removed. Then, ironically, just when the colonists and the British could finally breathe easily, the pleasant marriage between Britain and the colonies became a very messy divorce.

Trade and commerce with the American colonies was of great importance to Britain.

PART I: THE REVOLUTION

THE ORIGINS OF THE REVOLUTION

Pontiac (c. 1720–69) and other Native Americans hoped for French aid to support their rebellion, but it never came.

Rivals for Empire

The British colonies hugged the Atlantic coast. French colonies hemmed them in to the north and west. Spanish Florida did the same to the south. Britain, France and Spain struggled against each other for greater power in Europe – and in the Americas.

In the 1750s, Britain and France went to war. This conflict, called the Seven Years War in Europe, eventually included Spain as well. (The British colonists named it the French and Indian War.) The war began badly for the British, but ended well. The 1763 treaty that ended the fighting gave Britain control over the entire eastern third of North America. Ominously for the British, the French would not forget their defeat. Moreover, blending French and British colonies would be a challenge. Keeping peace with the Native Americans would be difficult as well.

Pontiac's Rebellion

Native Americans living around the Great Lakes did not want British rule. An Ottawa chief named Pontiac united several tribes in an effort to push the British out. In May 1763, he launched several attacks. The British rallied and Pontiac and his allies were forced to accept British rule.

The rebellion did, however, bring home to the British that they had a problem. If the colonists began to move west of the Appalachian Mountains, as they wanted to, fighting with Native Americans was inevitable. The British would have to send more soldiers. As a consequence, the British government decided to ban colonists from these lands. In the Proclamation of 1763, it set aside the lands west of the Appalachians for Native Americans. Colonists bristled – they were being prevented from moving where they wished.

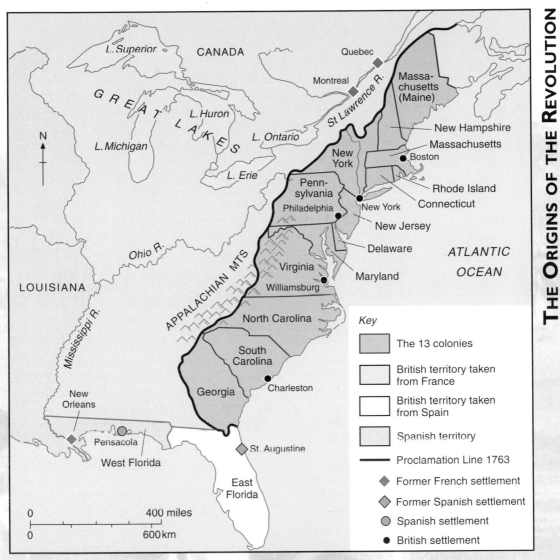

A map of North America, 1763. In winning the Seven Years War, Great Britain eliminated France from North America.

Map labels:

L. Superior · CANADA · Quebec
Montreal
L. Huron · Massa-chusetts (Maine)
L. Ontario · St Lawrence R.
N
L. Michigan · New Hampshire
GREAT LAKES · Massachusetts
L. Erie · New York · Boston
Penn-sylvania · Rhode Island
Philadelphia · New York · Connecticut
Ohio R. · New Jersey
Delaware · ATLANTIC OCEAN
APPALACHIAN MTS · Virginia · Maryland
LOUISIANA · Williamsburg
North Carolina
Mississippi R. · South Carolina
New Orleans · Georgia · Charleston
Pensacola
West Florida · St. Augustine
East Florida

0   400 miles
0   600 km

Key
- The 13 colonies
- British territory taken from France
- British territory taken from Spain
- Spanish territory
- Proclamation Line 1763
- ◆ Former French settlement
- ◆ Former Spanish settlement
- ● Spanish settlement
- ● British settlement

A Bitter Pill

The British government felt that its 3,755 troops in the colonies were too few. It decided to double the number of soldiers. Colonists feared that this larger army could be used against them. For the British, extra troops would increase costs. In 1763, George Grenville, the Prime Minister, sought to find the needed money but his solutions angered the colonists.

In 1764, Parliament placed duties on several goods imported into the colonies. It also changed the duty on imported molasses (a syrup made by refining sugar, used to make rum). Since the 1730s, the duty had been high, so colonial merchants ignored it, which the British allowed. Grenville's idea was to lower the duty so that colonial merchants would actually pay it.

Colonial Protest

The new law, which the colonists called the Sugar Act, angered Americans. Businessmen who made rum thought the tax was still too high. The stronger protest, though, focused on a statement in the Act. The offending phrase said that the law was being made because,

it is just and necessary, that a revenue be raised in your Majesty's said dominions in America.

In the past, the British had imposed duties to control commerce. Colonists had no objection to such laws. The Sugar Act, though, aimed to raise money. The colonists resented the change.

Taxation Without Representation

At a Boston town meeting, lawyer James Otis explained why. He drew on the Enlightenment idea that government was formed to benefit the governed. He praised the virtues of the British Constitution. Then he drew a principle from that Constitution. He said:

No parts of His Majesty's dominions can be taxed without consent.

To the British, the sugar duty was a matter of justice. They felt that American colonists should pay for their own defence. Otis cloaked opposition to the tax in fine clothes. Americans were not objecting to having to pay a tax, he argued – instead they were standing up for their rights.

The Stamp Act

When it passed the Sugar Act, Parliament declared that it was planning to impose another tax, one on documents. Even the suggestion of this new tax raised the hackles of the colonists. The assemblies of several colonies sent word to Britain that they opposed it.

Grenville moved ahead anyway. Parliament passed the Stamp Act in March 1765. The law required colonists to buy an official stamp that would go on every legal or business document and every newspaper, book and advertisement.

The tax on molasses had affected only merchants. The taxes on wine and silk had touched only the wealthy. But the stamp tax hit virtually every colonist.

James Otis (1725–83), the brilliant lawyer of the early Revolution, suffered a tragic end. A head injury from a 1769 tavern brawl left him insane, and in 1783 he was killed by lightning.

Grenville had planned this deliberately – he wanted to create a widespread tax that could not be avoided. The effect, though, was to increase opposition to the tax.

The Colonies Organise

The colonists howled against the Stamp Act. They repeated the argument that Parliament did not have the power to impose a tax on the colonies. They also objected because prosecutions for failure to pay the tax would be handled in naval courts. They saw this as a loss of rights because cases would not be heard by juries.

The protest took four forms. First was the verbal protest. On 31 May 1765, the assembly in Virginia – the House of Burgesses – approved the Virginia Resolves. These statements said that only colonial assemblies, not Parliament, had the right to tax the colonies. In the following months, eight other colonies passed similar resolutions.

Second was action on the streets. Mobs attacked many tax collectors and their homes. By January 1766, all thirteen tax collectors had resigned.

Third was united action. In June, the Massachusetts assembly recommended that the colonies meet to co-ordinate their efforts against the tax. In October, delegates from nine of the thirteen colonies met in the Stamp Act Congress. This body sent petitions to King and Parliament asking that both the Stamp Act and the Sugar Act be repealed. For the first time, the colonies had acted together.

Fourth was an economic attack. Merchants joined in non-importation agreements, that is, they agreed not to import British goods, because to do so they would need to pay for the official stamps. Trade between Britain and the colonies dried up.

The Stamp Act sailed easily through Parliament, partly because the British had paid a similar tax since 1695.

The names of the merchants who did not sign non-importation agreements were published so that colonists could boycott them.

A LIST of the Names of those who AUDACIOUSLY continue to counteract the UNITED SENTIMENTS of the BODY of Merchants thro'out NORTH-AMERICA; by importing British Goods contrary to the Agreement.

John Bernard,
(In King-Street, almost opposite Vernon's Head.
James McMasters,
(On Treat's Wharf.
Patrick McMasters,
(Opposite the Sign of the Lamb.
John Mein,
(Opposite the White-Horse, and in King-Street.
Nathaniel Rogers,
(Opposite Mr. Henderson Inches Store lower End King-Street.
William Jackson,
At the Brazen Head, Cornhill, near the Town-House.
Theophilus Lillie,
(Near Mr. Pemberton's Meeting-House, North-End.
John Taylor,
(Nearly opposite the Heart and Crown in Cornhill.
Ame & Elizabeth Cummings,
(Opposite the Old Brick Meeting-House, all of Boston.
Israel Williams, Esq; & Son,
(Traders in the Town of Hatfield.
And, Henry Barnes,
(Trader in the Town of M

Parliament Giveth and Taketh Away

British businessmen responded just as the colonists had hoped they would. Merchants told Parliament that many of them faced ruin because they were losing American business. Parliament debated whether to repeal the tax. Grenville, no longer Prime Minister, attacked the Americans for their 'open rebellion' and argued the case for sending troops to enforce the law. William Pitt blasted the government for its botched policy. He urged that the tax be dropped, but raised another issue:

Let the sovereign authority of this country over the colonies be asserted in as strong terms as can be devised, and be made to extend to every point of legislation.

Pitt's idea caught hold. In mid-March, Parliament approved two measures. One repealed the Stamp Act. The other, the Declaratory Act, stated that Parliament had the power to make laws that would be binding on the colonies 'in all cases whatsoever'. Repeal delighted the colonists. The New York assembly even voted to erect a statue to honour King George III. But the happy mood did not last long.

The government's repeal of the Stamp Act in 1766 was not welcomed by many Britons. What is the attitude of this cartoonist?

Born into a prosperous family, Sam Adams (1722–1803) lost his money through poor business decisions.

Seaman Crispus Attucks, an African American, was one of the five colonists killed in the Boston Massacre.

The Townshend Acts

Charles Townshend, now leading the British government, still saw a need to fill the treasury. In June 1767, he won Parliament's support for new import duties on paper, glass, paint and tea and for tougher enforcement. Once again, the colonists rallied against the new taxes.

Working Together

Massachusetts led the way. Sam Adams pushed the colony's assembly to petition the King. It urged him to ask the assembly, not Parliament, to approve taxes for the colony. The assembly also sent a message, called the Circular Letter, to the other colonial assemblies. It suggested that the colonies meet again.

Merchants in every colony except New Hampshire joined in a new non-importation agreement. The ban was effective – imports dropped from £2.3 million in 1768 to £1.3 million in 1769. Meanwhile, in Boston, tension was building. Customs officials were prevented from collecting taxes. The royal governor of Massachusetts dissolved the colony's assembly because it would not cancel the Circular Letter. In October, two regiments of British troops marched into Boston to keep order.

Pressure was growing in Britain to repeal the Townshend Act. At the same time, the British did not want to appear weak. In early 1770, Frederick North, the new Prime Minister, agreed to drop most of the Townshend duties. He kept one duty, on tea, to make it clear that Parliament was the supreme power.

Meanwhile, the situation in Boston worsened. The presence of British troops was a growing irritant. On 5 March 1770, the ill-feeling boiled over. That day, a Boston mob jeered, taunted and harassed some British soldiers. One soldier accidentally fired his gun and the others then opened fire. Within minutes, three colonists were dead and several more wounded. (Two of the wounded later died.) To the British, the incident showed the danger of mob action. To the colonists, it was the 'Boston Massacre'.

After nailing the Stamp Act to a 'Liberty Tree', the angry colonists in this cartoon tar and feather a tax agent and pour British tea down his throat.

Tea Overboard

An uneasy quiet settled over the colonies. Still, colonial leaders kept working behind the scenes. They set up committees of correspondence to communicate with like-minded people in other towns and colonies.

In 1773, the pot began to boil again. The East India Company, a large British trading company based in India, was having serious financial problems. The company needed to sell its tea to avoid bankruptcy. Parliament passed the Tea Act. The new law gave the East India Company the right to sell tea directly in the American colonies. While the aim was simply to help the East India Company, the effect would be to take business away from American merchants.

That autumn, three ships bearing tea reached Boston. At a huge mass meeting of thousands, Bostonians voted to send the tea back to Britain. The colonial governor refused. About two weeks later, the colonists struck. Disguised as Native Americans, a group of colonists boarded the ships and dumped the tea chests into Boston harbour.

The British Strike Back

The 'Boston Tea Party' demonstrated colonists' opposition to the Tea Act. To the British, it was vandalism. One observer reported:

The determination to enforce obedience from the colonies to laws of revenue by the most powerful means seems as firm as possible, and ... the [government] appears stronger than I have ever known it.

In March 1774, Parliament responded with four new laws. Called the Coercive Acts, they aimed to force the colonists to obey the law. One closed Boston harbour to all trade. Another revoked the charter of Massachusetts, taking away the colony's form of self-government. The third prevented colonial courts from bringing royal officials to trial while the fourth required colonists to allow British soldiers to stay in their homes.

General Thomas Gage (1721–87) advised King George III to take a tough stance against the colonists.

The *Journal of the Proceedings of the First Continental Congress*, 1774. This Congress met for less than two months before sending its appeal to Britain.

The British also replaced the governor of Massachusetts with General Thomas Gage, the commander of all British forces in the colonies. In May, he landed in Boston with four regiments of soldiers.

The Quebec Act

In June, Parliament dismayed the American colonists again. The Quebec Act set new rules for governing the French areas Britain had won in 1763. It created a legislature of appointed, not elected, members. It also allowed Catholics to hold office, which they could not do in Britain or other British colonies.

The new law made sense for Quebec, where French Catholics lived. The colonists, however, viewed it with alarm. Mostly Protestants, they had no sympathy for Catholics. Moreover, the law extended the new policy to Illinois, where some French settlers lived. This made Catholicism acceptable on land that the American colonists saw as theirs. Colonists lumped the Quebec Act together with the Coercive Acts. They called these laws 'the Intolerable Acts'.

Congress Assembled

In September 1774, the First Continental Congress opened in Philadelphia. Fifty-six delegates from every colony except Georgia attended. The delegates endorsed the Suffolk Resolves, which had been passed by a Boston town meeting. These resolves declared that the Coercive Acts violated the British Constitution. They also urged the colonies to form and train militia units.

Later, the delegates also approved a statement to be sent to Britain spelling out what they were against – the Coercive Acts, the Quebec Act, British troops in colonial towns and the dissolving of colonial assemblies. It also declared what they were for – the right of assemblies, rather than Parliament, to impose taxes on the colonies. Finally, the delegates agreed to meet again in the spring if the situation had not changed. The ball was in Britain's court.

JOURNAL

OF THE

PROCEEDINGS

OF THE

CONGRESS,

Held at PHILADELPHIA,
September 5, 1774.

PHILADELPHIA:

Taxation and Representation

The irony underlying the disputes between the colonists and the British government was that both were working from the same principles – the ideas of John Locke. In his *Second Treatise of Government* (1690), Locke argued that any taxation was coercive because it involved taking someone's property. Still, he reasoned, governments must have the power to tax so they can carry out their duties. Citizens had a duty to pay their taxes, but taxation must be with the citizens' own consent, that is, the consent of the majority, giving it either by themselves, or by the representatives chosen by them.

John Locke (1632–1704) was a British philosopher of the Enlightenment whose influence on political thought extended to France and America.

The American View

To the colonists, Locke's meaning was clear. Since they had no representatives in Parliament, it had no legitimate authority to tax them. On the other hand, the legislative assemblies in each colony did have representatives that they had elected. As a result, it was these bodies that had the authority to create taxes. The colonists had the argument about Parliament both ways. First, they said that a Parliament without American members had no right to tax them. At the same time, they agreed that there were many practical reasons why Americans could not be represented. The Stamp Act Congress of 1765 summed up the case:

The people of these colonies are not, and, from their local circumstances, cannot be represented in the House of Commons in Great Britain.

The Americans protested against taxation without representation and rejected representation. This clever position gave Parliament few options. Only taxes passed by the colonial assemblies could be considered valid. Anything else was oppression.

The British View

The British view emphasised another of Locke's ideas – that Parliament is the supreme power in the land. Locke had written,

> *There can be only one supreme power, which is the legislative, to which all the rest are and must be subordinate.*

The British Parliament was the legislature that mattered. Parliament had every right to impose taxes on British citizens, wherever they lived. As Grenville put it:

> *If Great Britain, under any conditions gives up her right of taxation she gives up her right of sovereignty, which is inseparable from it.*

That is, a sovereign nation – one that has the right to make decisions for itself – must have the power to tax. As Locke pointed out, only with the power to tax can government carry out its duties. The argument over taxation was a matter of principle. But from the same principles, the British and Americans reached two very different conclusions.

'Liberty triumphant or the downfall of oppression'. How does this American cartoonist view the distance between Britain and the colonies?

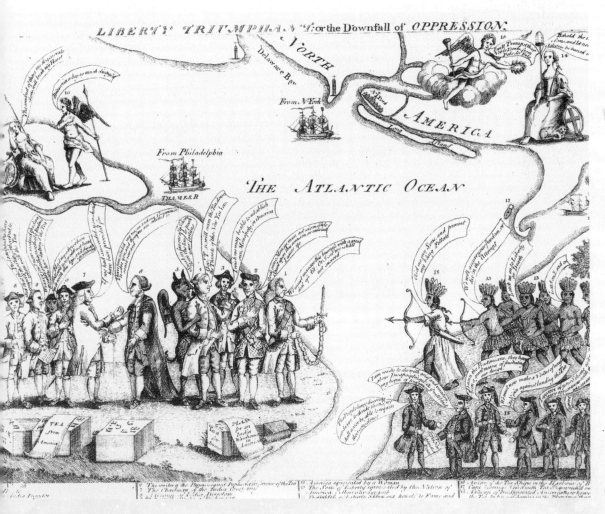

DECLARING INDEPENDENCE

William Pitt the Elder (1708–78) – his attempts at compromise were thwarted by Parliament.

The British Response

The message from the First Continental Congress found some receptive ears in London. William Pitt attempted to fashion a compromise. His plan was to grant official status to the Continental Congress in exchange for the colonists' agreement to any taxes. The colonists would also have to acknowledge that Parliament was the supreme legislative power. Whether the colonists would have accepted this plan will never be known, for Parliament rejected it.

Parliament aimed for a tough but friendly approach. It declared that Massachusetts was in a state of rebellion and banned the New England colonies from fishing in the Atlantic and from trading with anyone except Britain. On the other hand, it passed a law that removed all taxes except those that regulated trade. It also gave the colonial assemblies the task of raising taxes for the colonies' defence and for colonial government.

Taverns like this one in Boston, Massachusetts, were gathering places where colonists discussed politics.

Minutemen

The colonies, meanwhile, were preparing to fight. Rebels in Massachusetts formed a provisional government. It ordered the towns to train militia units. The troops were called 'Minutemen' because they were ready to fight at a moment's notice. Across New England, colonists raided British army arsenals, grabbing weapons and gunpowder.

'The Regulars Are Out'

In April 1775, General Thomas Gage received orders to enforce the Coercive Acts, with force if necessary. He was also told to halt the colonists' arms build-up. On the night of 18 April 1775, 700 British soldiers marched out of Boston for the town of Concord. They hoped to seize weapons and capture rebel leaders John Hancock and Sam Adams. The colonists knew the plans. Paul Revere and two others pounded down the roads from Boston to Concord on horseback. As he passed houses, Revere shouted, 'The regulars are out!' to tell the Minutemen to assemble. Reaching Concord, he urged Hancock and Adams to flee.

This romanticised version of the battle at Lexington shows the brave Minutemen – each clearly shown as an individual – facing a nameless body of Gage's British troops.

The War Begins

At Lexington, on the way to Concord, the British troops were met by about 70 Minutemen. A brief fight left eight Americans dead and ten wounded. Only one British soldier was hurt. The British marched on.

At Concord, a stronger American force attacked. The colonists fired on the British all the way back to Boston. In the end, the British had 73 soldiers killed, 26 missing and 174 wounded. The colonists had 49 killed, 5 missing and 41 wounded. The battles of Lexington and Concord, though small, were momentous. Talk had turned to war.

Congress Divided

New England militia set up camp outside Boston and began a siege of the British in the town. Gage defiantly declared martial law in Massachusetts, but he and his troops could not leave the city.

In mid-May, delegates gathered again in Philadelphia. The meeting, the Second Continental Congress, was attended by members from all thirteen colonies. The delegates heard about Lexington and Concord. They also learned that militia units had captured two British forts on New York's Lake Champlain. One, Fort Ticonderoga, yielded a rich store of guns and supplies.

The Congress had no legal authority to do anything. On the other hand, there seemed to be a war developing, so it decided to organise the army. In June, Congress voted to raise troops. It accepted control of the army outside Boston, and it chose George Washington to command the Continental Army.

John Adams of Massachusetts, who had nominated Washington, wanted a Virginian to command the New England army. He thought that would keep the colonies united. Washington took the post humbly:

I ... declare with the utmost sincerity, I do not think myself equal to the command I am honoured with.

Ethan Allen (1738–89) captured Fort Ticonderoga 'in the name of the Great Jehovah and the Continental Congress!' Many of the soldiers, including the commander, were awakened by the attack.

George Washington (1732–99) took command of the army on 3 July 1775.

Given his past record, he might have been correct. While in the Virginia militia, he had never won a battle. Still, he was a wise choice. Mature, honourable and dedicated, he would never shirk his duty or challenge civilian authority.

A Bloody Battle

Before Washington arrived to take command, the Americans and British fought a fierce battle known as the Battle of Bunker Hill (it was actually fought on Breed's Hill). About 1,500 colonists were dug in behind a hastily-made fort at the top of the hill. On the morning of 17 June, British ships opened fire on the fort. The shells fell short, however. In the afternoon, about 2,400 British troops landed. They charged the hill three times. The first two assaults were beaten back. The third succeeded when the colonists ran out of ammunition. The British captured both hills.

The Americans had 140 dead and 310 wounded, but they inflicted heavy losses on the British with more than 220 killed and more than 800 wounded. One British officer wrote angrily:

From an absurd and destructive confidence, carelessness or ignorance, we have lost a thousand of our best men and officers and have given the rebels great matter of triumph by showing them what mischief they can do us.

John Trumbull's famous painting of Bunker Hill shows (bottom left) the death of Dr Joseph Warren, one of the American militia commanders.

An Olive Branch

Congress, meanwhile, was stewing over what to do. At this point, only the most extreme delegates wanted independence. Most wanted to stay within the British Empire, but to be free of parliamentary control. The moderates won the day. In July, Congress approved a conciliatory petition to Britain. Since their quarrel was with Parliament, they addressed their petition to King George III.

The Olive Branch Petition asked the King to halt the fighting until the two sides could reach an agreement. Congress grandly declared that the colonists were of,

one mind resolved to die freemen, rather than to live like slaves.

Then it reassured the King that,

we mean not to dissolve that union which has so long and so happily subsisted between us.

On the other hand, Congress also rejected Lord North's conciliation plan.

Hardening the Lines

The King, in turn, wanted none of Congress. In August, he rejected the Olive Branch Petition, unread. He also declared that the colonies were in rebellion.

In the autumn of 1775, Congress issued a tough response. It approved an attempt to capture Canada. In November, the invading force captured Montreal. The attack on Quebec failed though, and the American army eventually withdrew.

George III (1738–1820) became King in 1760 – just before the troubles with the colonies began.

Where Colonists Stood

It is difficult to determine where most colonists stood on the question of independence in 1775. Some Loyalists felt that the conflict was the colonists' fault. Some colonists, loyal to the King, objected to many actions taken by his government. And some colonists were ready to separate from Britain. Over time, that number grew.

People in New England were generally the most ready for independence. Virginia was the most extreme of the Southern colonies, but in the South there tended to be differences by region. Planters and lawyers who lived near the coast were more radical. Small farmers in the backcountry were often Loyalists.

As well as exercising a great influence on the American revolutionaries, Thomas Paine (1737–1809) later wrote works in favour of the French Revolution and became a famous figure in Paris.

The Propaganda War

Writer Thomas Paine, who firmly opposed British rule, was determined to sway opinion. In January 1776, he published a skilfully written pamphlet called *Common Sense*. In it, he analysed how the British government had trampled on American rights. Pointing to recent battles, he concluded that,

About 30,000 German soldiers fought for the British during the revolutionary war.

> *reconciliation is now a fallacious [false] dream.*

The only answer, the common sense answer, he argued, was independence. Paine's pamphlet had impact. Washington said,

> *'Common Sense' is working a powerful change in the minds of men.*

Its popularity is suggested by its sales – 150,000 copies is an impressive total in a land of only about two million people.

The King's rejection of the Olive Branch Petition also moved many colonists towards independence, as did news that the British were hiring mercenaries from Germany. If the King hired foreign troops to shoot at his subjects, what chance was there of reconciliation?

Evacuation

Meanwhile, General Gage was reading the handwriting on the wall. In January, soldiers brought Washington cannons captured from Fort Ticonderoga. When his army forced the British off hills south of Boston, the cannons were used to bombard the British. Soon after, the British evacuated Boston. About 1,000 Loyalists also left the town.

Forming New Governments

By late spring 1776, John Adams had concluded that the colonies needed to separate from Britain. In May, he convinced Congress to suggest that each colony form a new government. Still, Adams felt he could not propose independence as he feared conservatives would defeat it. Since New England was seen as the home of radicals, he needed a colony outside New England to propose the idea.

Help came from the South. In mid-May the rebels in Virginia decided to back independence. As a result, Richard Henry Lee of Virginia introduced a resolution in Congress on 7 June, that,

These united colonies are, and of right ought to be, free and independent states ... and that all political connection between them and the state of Britain is, and ought to be, totally dissolved.

Adams wanted a unanimous vote, but the debate showed that some colonies still opposed the idea. As a result, he agreed to postpone the vote. In the meantime, Congress named a committee to write a declaration justifying independence, just in case! Adams was on that committee as was the highly-respected Benjamin Franklin of Pennsylvania. The most important member, though, was Thomas Jefferson. With a reputation for eloquent writing, Jefferson took on the task of writing the Declaration of Independence.

The Declaration

The document Jefferson wrote has resonated through the ages. The opening explained why the Declaration was written. 'A decent respect for the opinions of mankind' forces Congress to detail why it is taking such a step. The second section used the ideas of John Locke to explain the principles the colonists believed in:

Benjamin Franklin (left) of Pennsylvania and John Adams (centre) of Massachusetts review the draft Declaration of Independence written by Thomas Jefferson (standing) of Virginia.

We hold these truths to be self-evident, that all men are created equal, that they are endowed by their Creator with certain unalienable rights, that among these are life, liberty and the pursuit of happiness. That to secure these rights, governments are instituted among men, deriving their just powers from the consent of the governed. That whenever any form of government becomes destructive of these ends, it is the right of the people to alter or to abolish it, and to institute new government.

The Declaration was adopted on 4 July 1776 but not signed until 2 August, when a fair copy inscribed on parchment was available.

The third section was a list of charges against the King (not against Parliament). After George III rejected the Olive Branch Petition, he became the enemy. It was the tyranny of the King that Jefferson blamed for the need to break away from British rule. The purpose of this third section was to make the case that the King had violated his duty to protect the colonists' rights hence justifying the colonists' declaration of independence.

The Debate and the Decision

After Adams and Franklin had made minor changes to Jefferson's work, it was ready for Congress. First, though, the issue of independence itself had to be decided. In the passing days, Adams and his allies worked hard to persuade the other colonies to back independence. On 2 July, twelve colonies approved the resolution, with New York the lone holdout. Its assembly had instructed its delegates not to approve independence, but less than two weeks later, it voted for independence as well.

John Adams wrote that,

the greatest question was decided which ever was decided in America.

He went on to predict that 2 July,

will be celebrated by succeeding generations as the great anniversary festival … [The day] ought to be solemnised with pomp and parade, with shows, games, sports, guns, bells, bonfires and illuminations, from one end of the continent to the other.

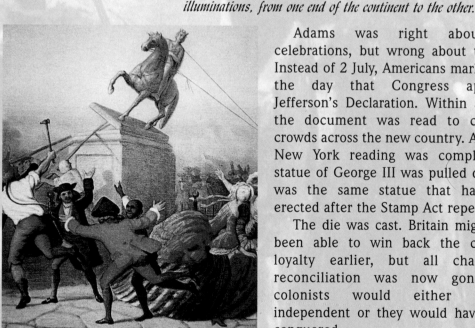

The two tons of lead in New York City's statue of George III were melted down to make musket balls.

Adams was right about the celebrations, but wrong about the day. Instead of 2 July, Americans mark 4 July, the day that Congress approved Jefferson's Declaration. Within a week, the document was read to cheering crowds across the new country. After the New York reading was completed, a statue of George III was pulled down. It was the same statue that had been erected after the Stamp Act repeal.

The die was cast. Britain might have been able to win back the colonies' loyalty earlier, but all chance of reconciliation was now gone. The colonists would either become independent or they would have to be conquered.

Good News

Soon after the approval of the Declaration, Congress received some good news – France and Spain had agreed to help the colonists. They did so to make life more difficult for Britain, their rival for power in Europe. Louis XVI of France granted the Americans $1 million worth of weapons. Spain donated aid as well.

Congress sent Franklin to France to win more aid. Delegates were dispatched to other countries.

The British Prosper

Meanwhile, the British amassed a huge force. Washington had guessed correctly that the British would move to New York. General William Howe began landing 32,000 troops on Staten Island on 2 July. His brother, Admiral Richard Howe, commanded a powerful fleet. It was not a good sign for the colonists.

In late August, the British won a smashing victory against the Americans on Long Island. Washington was forced to retreat. More bad news for the colonists came in October. A British fleet destroyed American ships on Lake Champlain. Just a few days later, Washington suffered defeat again at White Plains. Two weeks later, the colonists lost two forts near New York City. Washington was forced to retreat to Pennsylvania with Howe hot on his heels. Congress fled Philadelphia for safety.

In July 1776, the Second Continental Congress had boldly declared independence. Now, the colonists' army seemed about to lose it.

After victory at Long Island in August 1776, British troops paraded triumphantly through New York City.

'All Men Are Created Equal'

Before Congress approved Jefferson's Declaration, it made a few changes. The most important one was to remove a section about slavery and the slave trade. Jefferson had included these as examples of George III's crimes, but the Southern delegates were unwilling to condemn the institution on which their economy was based.

The irony of the slavery situation was not lost on Loyalists or the British. Congress had mightily declared that 'all men are created equal'. On the other hand, it was the colonists who kept slaves. As Dr Samuel Johnson, the famous British author, snorted in contempt:

How is it that we hear the loudest yelps for liberty among the drivers of Negroes?

James Armistead (right) spied for General Lafayette (left). At the French general's request, Virginia granted Armistead his freedom.

Some Progress?

To later generations, this apparent hypocrisy stains the Revolutionary cause. While slavery was not ended, the Revolution, and even Jefferson's Declaration, did benefit African Americans to some extent. Several states made it illegal to import slaves. Many who opposed slavery saw ending the slave trade as an important first step. The states that banned this trade included Virginia and Maryland – two states where slavery was well entrenched and an important part of the economy.

The six states of Pennsylvania, Massachusetts, Connecticut, Rhode Island, New York and New Jersey went further. By 1786, they had made slavery completely illegal. True, these changes were limited. Banning the slave trade did not free those who were already enslaved. Nor did it halt the growth of the number of slaves – the birth of each new generation brought more and more people into slavery. Moreover, slavery was completely banned only in Northern states where it had been less common in the first place.

Still, these acts were radical. Slavery had existed around the world for thousands of years. The ideology of the Revolution unquestionably led to these laws. Rhode Island clearly made the connection between its law banning slavery and the colonists' fight for freedom:

The implications of the Declaration were not lost on some states which banned the selling and transporting of slaves. However, slavery continued well into the next century.

Those who are desirous of enjoying all the advantages of liberty themselves should be willing to extend personal liberty to others.

The same was true in Massachusetts. Slavery was abolished there by the state court, based on the principle that the state's constitution – written by revolutionary John Adams – made slavery impossible when it declared 'all men are born free and equal'. While the new United States did not recognise the connection between this principle and the treatment of Africans, at least some states did.

WINNING INDEPENDENCE

Striking Back

The outlook was not brilliant for the American colonists towards the end of 1776. Tom Paine was inspired to write another pamphlet, *The American Crisis*. He tried hard to shore up the colonists' resolve:

These are the times that try men's souls. The summer soldier and the sunshine patriot will, in this crisis, shrink from the service of their country, but he that stands it now, deserves the love and thanks of man and woman.

By late December, about 1,200 British soldiers were stationed in Trenton, central New Jersey. Washington had a larger force across the river, but many were militia whose term to serve would end on 1 January. In addition, deserters were leaving his army every day. Washington knew he had to do something.

On 25 December, as the British celebrated Christmas, Washington's army crossed the Delaware River. Next morning, it struck. The surprise attack succeeded brilliantly. The Americans, at a cost of only four wounded, captured about 1,000 prisoners.

What qualities does the artist convey in this heroic portrayal of Washington crossing the Delaware River?

Winning New Jersey

General Howe, in New York, was outraged that British troops would surrender to 'a ragged and undisciplined militia' and immediately sent General Charles Cornwallis and a larger force down to New Jersey to meet Washington. The American commander, meanwhile, offered a $10 bounty to convince many of his militia to re-enlist.

Cornwallis and his 5,000 men arrived at Trenton and trapped Washington against the river. When the British commander decided to postpone his attack until the next day, Washington's army slipped away. Taking back roads to move north behind Cornwallis' line, their goal was the British supply depot in New Brunswick. On the way, Washington's army drove off a small British force at Princeton and forced the British to pull back. Too exhausted, though, to continue to New Brunswick, Washington and his forces took up winter quarters in Morristown. The British stayed in northern New Jersey. The battles of Trenton and Princeton had bought the Americans more time. In mid-March, Congress returned to Philadelphia. A few weeks later, it passed a law to create the first flag of the United States.

Attack from the North

In the spring of 1777, the British army launched two new assaults. Unfortunately, they were planned separately and were not co-ordinated. One was aimed at New York and the other, at Philadelphia.

The northern attack was led by General John Burgoyne. He planned to drive from Canada into New York so he could separate rebellious New England from the other colonies. In June 1777, Burgoyne set out from Canada with nearly 8,000 men. He captured Fort Ticonderoga in July, but his progress was then slowed by mountains and dense forests. By September, Burgoyne was just south of Saratoga, New York. There he found an American army.

The forces met on 19 September, fighting to a stand-off. The draw, however, favoured the Americans. They had held their ground against British regulars and were joined afterwards by more volunteers, swelling the American ranks. Burgoyne had no reinforcements. The two armies stayed in the area and waited.

The stars and stripes of the first official national flag were instituted on 14 June 1777. The Union is represented by thirteen white stars in a blue field 'representing a new constellation'.

Congress Flees

While Burgoyne was marching south, Howe left New York City. He hoped to capture Philadelphia by sea rather than marching across New Jersey. Had there been some communication, Howe could have stayed in New York and joined Burgoyne to destroy the American army at Saratoga. The British missed an opportunity.

Washington lost several battles to the British, including Brandywine, shown here. Can he be called a successful general?

Still, Howe enjoyed great success. In late August, he landed south-west of Philadelphia. Within days, his army defeated Washington's at the Battle of Brandywine. Soon after, the Continental Congress had to flee Philadelphia once again. American defeats at Paoli and Germantown followed. By late September, General Howe and his army held Philadelphia and its surroundings.

Stunning Upset

In October, Burgoyne's force tangled with the Americans once again. A young American general named Benedict Arnold led the army brilliantly to defeat the British. American General Horatio Gates took the credit, but Arnold had won the battle. (Later, Arnold changed sides. Disappointed by not being promoted, and in love with a Loyalist woman, he joined the British.)

When he surrendered to Gates, Burgoyne said, 'General, the caprice of war has made me your prisoner'.

Burgoyne was forced to retreat. Within days, his army was trapped against the Hudson River. On 17 October 1777, Burgoyne surrendered nearly 6,000 soldiers and almost 30 cannons. It was a stunning defeat for a force that Burgoyne had once called 'irresistible'.

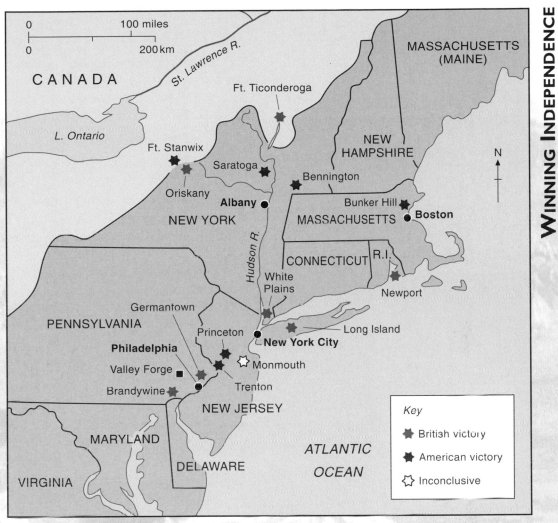

A map of the Northern campaigns from late 1776 to August 1778.

British Resolve, French Aid

When news of the surrender reached Britain, the government determined to carry on the war. Critics suggested repealing the laws that the Americans had objected to, but the idea was voted down. Instead, Parliament approved raising £13 million for the war effort.

When reports of Saratoga reached France, Franklin went to work. Soon after, France officially recognised the independence of the United States. Later, the two countries signed a treaty that made them allies. They pledged to continue fighting until American independence had been won. Each promised not to sign a treaty with Britain without the consent of the other. France agreed that any lands won from Britain in North America would belong to the United States. The treaty was a triumph for the Americans.

Chill in Pennsylvania

Diplomatic success came in the midst of difficult times. Washington and his army spent the winter of 1777–78 at Valley Forge, outside Philadelphia. It was a miserable winter. One soldier lamented,

The army at Valley Forge survived by eating 'firecakes' – flour and water cooked on hot stones.

Poor food – hard lodgings – cold weather – fatigue – nasty clothes – nasty cooking … I can't endure it – why are we sent here to starve and freeze – what sweet felicities have I left at home.

Desertions were common. Men and officers grumbled about Washington's leadership and a group of officers even joined with a few members of Congress to discredit Washington, hoping to have him relieved by General Horatio Gates, the self-proclaimed victor at Saratoga. The plot was uncovered, and Washington was left in command.

Steps were taken to improve the delivery of food and supplies. Parties began to seize livestock and food from Loyalist farms nearby. The soldiers survived the awful winter. Meanwhile, a German officer who served with the American army made the time spent at Valley Forge useful. Baron Friedrich von Steuben drilled the troops every day, taught them how to march and fight in formation, and instilled discipline. He turned a collection of farmers and labourers into an army.

Von Steuben spoke no English. He gave his orders in French and they were then translated.

The Peace Commission

When news of the French–American alliance reached Britain, the government made two decisions. First, it decided to pull the British army out of Philadelphia, and replace Howe with General Henry Clinton. Clinton was to take his force back to New York.

Second, the government decided to propose peace with an offer that would turn the clock back to 1763. The government would drop all the taxes and other Acts of Parliament that the colonists objected to. It would even give up the right to tax the colonies and consider bringing Americans into Parliament. The Americans, in turn, had to drop the claim of independence. The British hoped that the peace commissioners would reach the Continental Congress before the French treaty.

However, on 4 May, Congress signed the treaty with France. Washington's troops had weathered the winter, and new volunteers were swelling the army. Clinton's army was preparing to leave Philadelphia. Congress rejected the peace commissioners with bold words:

General Clinton (1738–95) chose to march across New Jersey from Philadelphia to New York. British ships were used to move about 3,000 Loyalists who left Philadelphia at the same time.

We are ready ... to enter upon the consideration of peace whenever the King of England should show us that he has any sincere disposition for that purpose. The only evidence of that sincerity would be an explicit acknowledgement of the independence of these states.

The Americans Rebound

Clinton marched his army to New York but the going was slow, and the army was vulnerable. Washington advanced through the centre of New Jersey and attacked the rear of Clinton's army at Monmouth. The Americans could have won the battle – they had a larger force in the area – but mismanagement led to a retreat that almost became a rout. Washington had to rally the soldiers to save the day.

After Monmouth, the British completed their move to New York. For the next two years, there were no major battles. Clinton remained cooped up in the city. He did not have enough soldiers to fight Washington on open ground. Washington, in turn, did not have enough manpower to attack Clinton. His main concern was simply to hold his army together.

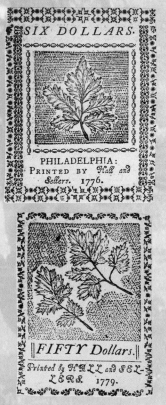

American paper money lost so much value that things of little merit were said to be 'not worth a Continental'.

Money Woes

During this stalemate, the Americans had plenty of problems. An important one was money. Printing presses kept churning out 'Continentals', as the new dollar bills were called, but Congress had no gold or silver to back them. As a result, the value of paper money plunged during the war. By 1779, a dollar was worth only ten cents.

The price of goods skyrocketed. Flour cost 2,000 per cent more in 1781 than it had in 1776. At the same time, consumers faced shortages. Merchants and shopkeepers also kept other goods off the market. Since prices were rising, they reasoned, it would be better to sell tomorrow than today. Farmers hid their livestock and food for fear that either army would simply take them.

Late in the war, Robert Morris took charge of the country's finances. Morris, a wealthy businessman, helped save the United States. He profited handsomely from this work, but without his efforts, the army could not have been paid or fed, and the new government would have collapsed.

Loyalists

Another problem for the rebels was the Loyalists. One estimate puts the number of Loyalists as high as 500,000 – more than twenty per cent of the population. They caused problems for the colonial armies – as many as 30,000 actively fought alongside the British during the war and those who did not fight could still report on the movements of Washington's soldiers. Loyalist farmers also gave supplies to the British and withheld them from the rebels.

Twice British strategy aimed at taking advantage of Loyalist support. When the British moved to Philadelphia in late 1777 and into the South in 1780, they hoped that large numbers of Loyalists in those areas would support the army. The support that arrived was never that great, though. However, when the British left an area, Loyalists followed. In the end, perhaps as many as 80,000 left the United States during and after the war.

The War Moves South

Another reason that the war moved south in 1780 was the idea that the now small British army could fare better in the less populous South than the more developed North. The British also hoped to encourage Southern slaves to escape to British lines thereby weakening their rebellious masters.

The Southern effort began in late 1779, when the British captured Savannah, Georgia. Clinton came south and took Charleston in May 1780. More than 5,000 American soldiers under General Benjamin Lincoln surrendered. Washington sent part of his army south, and Congress placed Gates in command. British troops under General Charles Cornwallis defeated the Americans at Camden, South Carolina – 900 Americans were killed and 1,000 prisoners taken. Gates' performance was so poor that he was replaced by General Nathanael Greene. Before Greene arrived, Cornwallis moved into North Carolina. American victories at Kings Mountain and Cowpens weakened his forces. He beat back the Americans at Guilford Courthouse, but the battle bloodied him. He retired to Wilmington, North Carolina, to await reinforcements.

A map of the Southern campaigns, from late 1779 to 1781.

N

APPALACHIAN MTS

Richmond

VIRGINIA

Yorktown

Guilford
Courthouse

NORTH CAROLINA

Cowpens

Kings
Mountain

Camden

SOUTH
CAROLINA

ATLANTIC
OCEAN

GEORGIA

Charleston

Savannah

Key

British victory

American victory

Inconclusive

0   100 miles
0   200 km

American Victory at Yorktown

A year later, Cornwallis launched a Virginia campaign. His 7,500-man army carried out raids, harassing the Americans wherever it could. By August 1781, Cornwallis had reached the town of Yorktown. It ended up being a poor position. American troops moved in quickly to contain him. Soon after, they were joined by French forces. In a September naval battle near Yorktown, the French defeated the British fleet, giving the allies control over the sea in the area. The British could not help Cornwallis' army escape or bring reinforcements. By late September, Washington reached the area with more troops. He had about 16,000 men compared to Cornwallis' 8,000.

From 9 October, the allies' cannon pounded the British day after day. Stormy weather foiled a British attempt to escape and on 19 October, Cornwallis surrendered.

As the British army surrendered at Yorktown in October 1781, the band played a tune called 'The World Turned Upside Down'.

The Peace Negotiations

Yorktown was the last major battle of the war. There were still skirmishes and the peace was not settled for nearly two years. However, Lord North's immediate response to the news of Yorktown – 'O God! It is all over!' – was accurate. On 27 February 1782, Parliament voted against continuing the war. On 5 March, it voted to begin peace negotiations with the United States.

Those talks took place in Paris. The American negotiator was Benjamin Franklin, later joined by John Adams and John Jay. Speaking for the British was Richard Oswald, a Scottish businessman who had once lived in Virginia. The Americans insisted that the British first recognise their independence. The British government, reluctantly, agreed to this step in September 1782.

The Treaty of Paris

The treaty was finalised by late November. Britain granted the United States all the land east of the Mississippi River except Florida (Florida and a strip of coastal land extending to the Mississippi went to Spain, which had entered the war against Britain in 1779). It agreed to allow Americans to fish in the waters of eastern Canada. The United States agreed that its citizens would repay debts owed to British merchants from before the war. It also promised to compensate Loyalists for property taken from them. Final acceptance of the treaty was delayed by a change of government in Britain. It was finally signed in Paris on 3 September 1783. The war was over.

On 5 December 1783, George III presented the terms of the Treaty of Paris to Parliament. To achieve 'reconciliation' with the colonies, he said, he was willing to 'declare them free and independent states'. A French observer noted,

In pronouncing 'independence' the King of England did it in a constrained voice.

This French allegory shows France sustaining America – an acknowledgement of French aid to the colonists.

A map of North America after the Treaty of Paris in 1783.

Key

American states

American territories

British holdings

Spanish holdings

Why the British Lost

When the Revolution began, Britain was a great power with an experienced army and a strong navy. It had economic resources and a King who was determined to keep the American colonies intact. The rebellious colonies had to unite disparate forces, form an army, create a government and find money for the whole effort. How, then, did Britain lose the war?

Military Problems

One set of reasons was military. The British never had a clear strategy for winning the war. They tried to punish the rebels but were unwilling to carry out wholesale destruction that would make the colonists drop their rebellion. At the same time, they could never completely destroy Washington's army. They spent long periods of time cooped up in the major cities of the North, unable to break out.

Supply and communication were also problems. British troops could not count on getting supplies from the American countryside and so were dependent on goods from overseas. Weeks or even months were needed to send messages from one side of the Atlantic to the other and as much time was needed for the response. As a result, plans were always based on outdated information.

Yet it was not just a question of British military weakness. Washington held his army together, avoiding disaster with the attack on Trenton, maintaining hope during the winter at Valley Forge, and saving the day at Monmouth. The French alliance, too, strengthened the Americans' hand with France providing valuable supplies, extra men and a useful navy.

The Americans also had an easier task in fighting the war. The British had to overcome the American army and convince the people to abandon independence. The Americans, on the other hand, simply had to survive, hoping that the British would give up.

Lack of Unity and Exhaustion

The British Parliament was not united behind the war effort. Some MPs had opposed the policies of the British government before the war, while some continued to criticise the conduct of the war. Moreover, as the conflict dragged on, many in Britain became fed up with it. Historian Edward Gibbon, who supported the war at first, later lost his desire to continue fighting:

> I shall never give my consent to exhaust still further the finest country in the world in this prosecution of a war from whence no reasonable man entertains any hope of success. It is better to be humbled than ruined.

This cartoon of 1782 is entitled 'Britannia and her Daughter America'.

THE CONFEDERATION GOVERNMENT

John Dickinson (1732–1808), while a lawyer by profession, first gained fame for his pamphlet, *Letters of a Farmer in Pennsylvania*.

Congress Creates a Government

While fighting the war, the Continental Congress also had to create a government. The work began in June 1776, even before independence was declared. On 11 June, Congress created a committee to draft the Declaration of Independence. The next day, it named another committee to draft a plan of government.

John Dickinson, author of the Olive Branch Petition, drafted the plan. Having undergone major changes, the final document came to be called the Articles of Confederation.

Powers of the Central Government

The Articles granted certain powers to the Congress. Chief among them was the power to wage war and make peace with foreign countries. The states still retained the power to take independent action with foreign powers.

Congress was also authorised to create a postal service and set standard weights and measures. It could coin and borrow money, but could not, however, impose taxes. It could only estimate the government's financial needs and ask the states to raise taxes to meet those needs.

Congress was the only branch of the national government. There was no executive power, like a state's governor. There were not even national courts.

Fear of Central Government

When the Articles were written, Americans wanted local government, not distant government. They saw themselves more as citizens of different states than as members of a nation. In addition, they had great mistrust of central government. The tyranny of Britain's central government, they believed, was the source of their problems. They were hardly willing to create a powerful national government.

Congress hoped to ensure each state's ability to run its own affairs. The second of the thirteen Articles sharply limited the power of the central government:

Each state retains its sovereignty, freedom and independence, and [reserves] every power, jurisdiction and right, which is not by this confederation expressly delegated to the United States, in Congress assembled.

Several states claimed land all the way to the Mississippi River.

Stumbling Blocks

STATE CLAIMS
TO
WESTERN LANDS
1783-1802

Scale of Miles
0   100   200   300   400

Though the Articles were drafted by July 1776, more than a year was needed to approve them. Four main issues held up this approval. One was the relative power of the central and state governments. The second was the thorny issue of representation. In the end, each colony had an equal vote. Third was the cost of the war. The delegates finally agreed that this cost was a national responsibility. Since Congress had no power to impose taxes, though, such words were empty.

Finally, there came the most contentious question of western lands. Eight states claimed lands west of the Appalachian Mountains. Those that did not thought the western lands should be controlled by the national government. The states with these claims disagreed, not surprisingly. This issue held up final ratification for many months.

Ratifying the Articles

In November 1777, the Continental Congress finally hammered out an approved version of the Articles of Confederation. For the plan to take effect, the state legislatures had to approve it. Twelve states quickly did so. Maryland held out because of the western lands issue. Finally, the eight states yielded their claims to the national government. Once they did, Maryland ratified. The Articles of Confederation went into effect in March 1781.

Foreign Challenges

In 1783, the United States signed the Treaty of Paris with Britain. The war was over, and independence was won, but serious problems remained. Most important were challenges from foreign powers and financial troubles.

The Treaty of Paris required Britain to abandon its forts in the western lands. British soldiers stayed, however, and they had a ready excuse – Americans had not met their own treaty obligations. After all, debtors were not paying the money they owed to British merchants, and Loyalists were not being compensated for lost property. The British said that until these problems were resolved, they would not leave the forts.

The Treaty of Paris, 1783, was a triumph for the Americans, but was not without consequent problems.

The other dispute was with Spain. Spain held lands west of the Mississippi River and the key port of New Orleans near its mouth. The Spanish felt threatened by the United States and began to flex their muscles.

They closed the Mississippi to Americans, a step that hurt Americans living beyond the Appalachians. The river, after all, was the easiest route for them to ship their goods to market. Without access to the river, they would have to haul their products over the mountains.

John Jay worked out a treaty with Spain that regained Americans' access to the river, but at a high price. The United States had to give up its claim to the river for 25 years. Northern members of Congress agreed. Those in the South, though, resented it bitterly. They had closer ties to the western settlers and saw Jay's work as willingness to throw aside the rights of those settlers.

As a result, the treaty was never approved. The real effect, though, was to drive a wedge between the Northern and Southern members of Congress – a wedge that helped weaken the national government.

John Jay (1745–1829) had been appointed secretary of foreign affairs on his return from negotiating the Treaty of Paris.

The Land Ordinance set surveyors to work in the north-western lands.

Orderly Transition

The Confederation Congress had two important successes. In 1785, it approved the Land Ordinance. This law established how the lands north of the Ohio River would be disposed of. It provided for surveying the land, dividing it into townships and selling most of it at only $1 per acre.

Two years later, Congress passed the Northwest Ordinance. This law created a territorial government for this area. It also spelled out the steps territories needed to follow to become states. With this act, Congress ensured that the United States could grow.

The Northwest Ordinance also banned slavery from these lands. This step helped solidify the economic and social differences that divided North and South. The North relied on free labour, and the South on slave labour. The ban on slavery meant these differences would carry into the western lands as they were settled.

Money Woes

Congress had experienced great difficulty raising money to carry on the war. It tried to create a duty on imports in 1781, but the states never approved the plan. It tried again in 1783, hoping to raise money to pay off the war debt. Again, the states did not approve the tax.

Financial worries topped the list of Congress' problems. The nation's economy stumbled when the war ended. Lack of production left people unemployed and cut into tax revenues. In addition, the government had to repay the money it had borrowed to fight the war. Complicating matters was the fact that states could issue their own money and follow their own financial policies.

Shays' Rebellion

In the mid-1780s, farmers in Massachusetts were being squeezed. They owed money and taxes, but had little cash. In the summer of 1786, farmers in the western part of the state began an armed revolt and closed the

A mob of Massachussetts farmers took possession of a courthouse during Shays' Rebellion.

courts. Their goal was simple – they wanted to keep their land. With the courts closed, banks could not carry out foreclosures or seize their property for failure to make mortgage payments.

By the winter of 1787, about 3,000 farmers were rebelling. Their leader was Daniel Shays. Like many of these farmers, he had fought in the Revolutionary war. The state sent a militia army to suppress the rebellion. It captured the farmers, putting an end to the protest, but many in the state felt sympathetic to the rebels. That autumn, voters elected a new state government, which pardoned all the participants. Still, the underlying problems remained. Shays' Rebellion had thrown a scare into many American leaders. George Washington summed up the feeling. Writing to James Madison, he said,

We are fast verging to anarchy and confusion.

A proclamation by Governor James Bowdoin of Massachusetts in September 1786 to 'prevent and suppress all such violent and riotous proceedings'.

Call to Order

Madison agreed. Like many others, he thought that the central government was too weak. In early 1786, he had persuaded the legislature of Virginia to suggest a meeting of all the states. The meeting took place at Annapolis, Maryland, in September 1786. Delegates from only five states attended, however.

The delegates knew they could not act for the whole country, but they felt that action was needed. They called for another meeting the following May and urged all the states to attend. Their worry was shown in the agenda they set for this meeting:

To devise such further provisions as shall appear ... necessary to render the constitution of the Federal Government adequate to the exigencies of the Union.

Once Shays' Rebellion broke out, an anxious Congress joined in the call for a meeting.

Commonwealth of Massachusetts.

By His EXCELLENCY

JAMES BOWDOIN, Esquire,

Governour of the Commonwealth of Massachusetts.

A Proclamation.

WHEREAS information has been given to the Supreme Executive of this Commonwealth, that on Tuesday last, the 29th of August, being the day appointed by law for the fitting of the Court of Common Pleas and Court of General Sessions of the Peace, at Northampton, in the county of Hampshire, within this Commonwealth, a large concourse of people, from several parts of that county, assembled at the Court-House in Northampton, many of whom were armed with guns, swords and other deadly weapons, and with drums beating and fifes playing, in contempt and open defiance of the authority of this Government, did, by their threats of violence and keeping possession of the Court-House until twelve o'clock on the night of the same day, prevent the fitting of the Court, and the orderly administration of justice in that county:

AND WHEREAS this high-handed offence is fraught with the most fatal and pernicious consequences, must tend to subvert all law and government; to dissolve our excellent Constitution, and introduce universal riot, anarchy and confusion, which would probably terminate in absolute despotism, and consequently destroy the fairest prospects of political happiness, that any people was ever favoured with

I HAVE therefore thought fit, by and with the advice of the Council, to issue this Proclamation, calling upon all Judges, Justices, Sheriffs, Constables, and other officers, civil and military, within this Commonwealth, to prevent and suppress all such violent and riotous proceedings, if they should be attempted in their several counties

AND I DO hereby, pursuant to the indispensible duty I owe to the good people of this Commonwealth, most solemnly call upon them, as they value the blessings of freedom and independence, which at the expence of so much blood and treasure they have purchased—as they regard their faith, which in the fight of GOD and the world, they pledged to one another, and to the people of the United States, when they adopted the present Constitution of Government—as they would not disappoint the hopes, and thereby become contemptible in the eyes of other nations, in the view of whom they have risen to glory and empire—as they would not deprive themselves of the security derived from well-regulated Society, to their lives, liberties and property; and as they would not devolve upon their children, instead of peace, freedom and safety, a state of anarchy, confusion and slavery,—I do most earnestly and most solemnly call upon them to aid and assist with their utmost efforts the aforesaid officers, and to unite in preventing and suppressing all such treasonable proceedings, and every measure that has a tendency to encourage them.

GIVEN at the COUNCIL-CHAMBER, in Boston, this second day of September, in the year of our Lord, one thousand seven hundred and eighty-six, and in the eleventh year of the Independence of the United States of AMERICA

JAMES BOWDOIN.

By his Excellency's command

JOHN AVERY, jun. Secretary.

BOSTON: Printed by ADAMS and NOURSE, Printers to the GENERAL COURT.

Henry Laurens, Virginia planter and president of Congress in 1777 and 1778. The Articles government he presided over had limited long-term potential.

The Weaknesses of the Confederation

The government created by the Articles of Confederation won the war. It could not solve the problems that plagued the new nation, though, as it had several weaknesses.

Those weaknesses were the result of key decisions made in writing the Articles. In creating the Articles government, delegates were reacting to recent history. They sharply remembered the arguments over the legitimate powers of Parliament. They had no desire to create a national government that could – as they felt Parliament clearly had – abuse its power and trample their rights. As a result, they crafted a document that placed the lion's share of power in the hands of the states, not the national government.

The first weakness was the most basic. The power of the national government was severely limited. Recall Locke's argument that the power to tax was fundamental to any government – without that power, the government could not carry out its plans. That is precisely the way that the Articles restricted the national government. Congress did not have the power to tax. It could merely send requests to the states for money. The state legislatures could refuse to provide the needed funds. If they refused – and they often did – the states could block Congress.

In addition, each state enjoyed too much power to make its own decisions. States could – and did – coin their own money. In addition, though Congress could regulate trade between states, its laws would not take effect if they ran counter to state laws. As a result, states effectively controlled this trade. These provisions made it difficult to carry on business between states. States' power to regulate trade even extended to trade with foreign countries. Any commercial treaties that Congress made with foreign countries could be limited by state laws. With no power to enforce its treaties, Congress had difficulty getting Britain, Spain, and other nations to sign such treaties. At any rate, those other powers, particularly Britain, had little interest in doing anything to help the American economy recover from the war.

Moreover, the various regions of the country had different societies, economies and interests. Each state or region could act in its own narrow self-interest. Since the national government was weak, it was unable to reconcile those differences or force the states to look to the broader national interest. In addition, a very few states could block action by Congress. The votes of nine states were needed to approve a law – thus only five states were required to block a law from passage.

The conflict with British colonial rule had led to other decisions that had weakened the Articles government. Royal governors and the King had wielded the executive power during colonial times. To the colonists, that power was often abused. While the state constitutions created governors, whose power was often limited by the power of other branches of the government, the creators of the national government feared such power on a national scale.

As a result, they created no executive power. That meant that no one person or small group of people could respond quickly to a crisis, such as Shays' Rebellion. A nine-state majority was needed to make every decision. In addition, members of Congress had to assume all the duties of executive branches, overseeing the treasury, diplomacy, defence and so on. Members could become overworked. Disagreements among members could prevent effective action. The national government also had no courts. There was no clear way of resolving disputes between states.

Inflexibility

Finally, the Articles were nearly impossible to change. A unanimous vote by all the state legislatures was needed to approve any amendments to the basic law. It was unlikely that the states would completely agree on anything. This last weakness, in fact, helped bring about the end of the Articles government. If it had been easier to change the Articles, the Constitutional Convention might never have met. But the men who met in Philadelphia in 1787 did not believe that they could fix the Articles. Instead, they threw them overboard and wrote a new framework of government.

A NEW GOVERNMENT

The Men of the Convention

The Constitutional Convention began to gather in Philadelphia in mid-May 1787. James Madison arrived first, and was the driving force behind the movement to write a new framework of government. Eventually, there were 55 delegates from every state except Rhode Island.

The delegates were men of property and experience. There were no women, no African Americans, and no poor people or even small farmers. Several delegates had large landholdings, and nineteen owned slaves. Many had served in the Continental Congress, state governments or both. Some had fought in the army. Most were in their thirties or forties, but 81-year-old Benjamin Franklin took part as well. A large number were lawyers.

Some talented leaders were absent. John Adams, Thomas Jefferson and John Jay were all representing the United States in Europe. Patrick Henry and Sam Adams were not present either because they were opposed to a stronger central government.

The Convention met for nearly five months during a hot, humid Philadelphia summer. Despite the heat, the windows were shut tight. One of the earliest decisions was to make the debates secret. This allowed the delegates to speak frankly and to explore the various proposals fully. Of course, it also shut the public out of their decisions completely.

The Man of the Hour

Another early decision was to make Washington the president of the Convention. After the war, Washington was 51 years of age and war weary. Fearing that the Articles government was too weak though, he had responded to Madison's pleas to come out of retirement. His presence underscored the seriousness of the situation.

Complete faith in Washington explains why he was unanimously chosen as president. During the debates, he was impartial but, behind the scenes, he worked to win approval for the new plan of government.

James Madison (1751–1836) was only 36 when he helped forge the Constitution. He had already been involved in government for ten years.

In this painting, Washington (standing, right) accepts the signed Constitution. The Constitution was debated and written in the same Philadelphia room where the Declaration of Independence had been approved.

Central Questions

The Virginians had met before the meeting and discussed a plan Madison had drafted. On 29 May, Edmund Randolph introduced it. The Virginia Plan called for a strong national government with a two-house legislature. There would also be an executive power headed by several officials and a judiciary. The upper house of the legislature would name the people to fill the executive and judgeships.

The purpose of the meeting had been, on the surface, to fix problems with the Articles. Accepting the Virginia plan would mean overthrowing them. The Convention faced a crucial decision. Within days, the delegates agreed to the idea of three branches of government. With that, it was clear that the Articles of Confederation were being abandoned. The debate that followed centred on six issues. In each, the delegates wrestled with key questions.

Many States or One Nation?

The first issue was how strong the central government should be. Madison, Washington and others were convinced that the government created by the Articles was far too weak. As Washington had written before the Convention began:

 The consequences of ... [an] inefficient government are too obvious to be dwelt upon. Thirteen sovereignties pulling against each other, and all tugging at the federal head, will soon bring ruin upon the whole.

The US Capitol, where Congress meets, was first erected in 1793, but had to be rebuilt after destruction by fire in the War of 1812.

Federalism

The Convention decided to create a federal system. In such a system, the national and state governments divide power. The national, or federal, government was given certain powers. Some were those that the Congress, under the Articles, had enjoyed, such as the power to wage war and make peace. Others were new. The national government under the Constitution, for example, had the power to regulate trade among the states. Only the national government, not the states, could coin money. The states reserved those powers not explicitly given to the federal government. States, for example, could oversee education and regulate business within their borders.

Some powers were shared. Both the states and the national government had the power to raise taxes. This, of course, was an important change from the Articles.

States or People?

While the delegates agreed on a stronger national government, they were divided on how to balance the power of the states. The Virginia Plan had two houses in the legislature. In both, the number of representatives each state had would be based on the state's population. Thus, large states would have more members than small states. James Wilson of Pennsylvania defended this plan:

 Can we forget for whom we are forming a government? Is it for men, or for the imaginary beings called states?

The small states wanted to keep the equality that they enjoyed under the Articles. This was called the New Jersey Plan. Connecticut's Oliver Ellsworth explained this position:

> *No instance of a confederacy has existed in which an equality of voices has not been exercised by the members of it.*

This was the most divisive issue of the Convention. It was also tied to another – how members would be chosen for these two houses. In the Virginia Plan, members of the lower house would be elected by the people. Those in the upper house would be chosen by the lower house. Here, the issue was whether to trust the people. The framers of the Constitution feared mob rule if democracy was too widespread. Elbridge Gerry of Massachusetts said,

> *The evils we experience flow from the excess of democracy.*

Two Houses

The final answer was a compromise suggested by Roger Sherman of Connecticut. The delegates chose to have two houses with members chosen in two different ways. In the lower chamber, the House of Representatives, the number of members was based on each state's population. Members of the House were elected directly by the people. In the upper chamber, the Senate, each state had an equal share of power, with two senators. Members of the Senate were originally chosen by the state legislatures. (A 1913 amendment made them directly elected.)

North or South?

A related debate was whether to count slaves when determining representation. This would have direct impact on regional power in the House. If slaves were counted, the Southern states would have larger populations and thus more representatives. If not, the Northern states would have more power, and the Southern states would probably reject the new plan.

Should slaves be counted? Slavery and the slave trade became an issue about representation when the convention debated the new Constitution.

TO BE SOLD. on board the Ship *Bance-Island*, on tuesday the 6th of *May* next, at *Afhley-Ferry*; a choice cargo of about 250 fine healthy NEGROES, juſt arrived from the Windward & Rice Coaſt. —The utmoſt care has already been taken, and ſhall be continued, to keep them free from the leaſt danger of being infected with the SMALL-POX, no boat having been on board, and all other communication with people from *Charles-Town* prevented.
Auſtin, Laurens, & Appleby.

N. B. Full one Half of the above Negroes have had the SMALL-POX in their own Country.

Sowing the Wind

The Convention compromised again. To save the Constitution, it entrenched slavery. First, it agreed to count each slave as three-fifths of a person for the sake of representation. (This provision became void when slavery was abolished by the Thirteenth Amendment in 1865.) It also agreed to prevent the new Congress from banning the import of slaves until 1808. Madison bitterly opposed the idea, but made clear why he was willing to support it:

 Great as the evil is, a dismemberment of the union would be worse.

It would take a long, bloody and bitter war to finally eliminate slavery. In the 1780s, though, these men were more concerned with ensuring the nation's survival.

Tyrant or Saviour?

Another concern was the character and nature of the executive. The Virginia Plan suggested an executive branch that included more than one person. This reflected many delegates' fear that a single executive would be like a monarchy, which could easily descend into a tyranny. Some thought the American people would never accept a single executive. As Randolph said:

 The permanent temper of the people was adverse to the very semblance of monarchy.

Creating the Presidency

James Wilson pointed out that every state had a single executive, a governor. The delegates agreed and voted for a single executive. Supporting Wilson's argument was their faith in Washington. It was widely understood that he would be the first president. The delegates knew they could trust him not to abuse the power of the office.

To be safe, the delegates also limited the president's power. First, the term of office was only four years. Second, although the president had the power to veto any act of Congress, Congress could override that veto. Third, a vote in the Senate was needed to confirm the president's appointment of judges and top advisors. Also, judges the president named served for life, making them independent of him. Finally, Congress was given the power to remove a president from office if it decided that he or she committed 'high crimes and misdemeanours'.

The impeachment trial of Bill Clinton in 1999 in the chamber of the United States Senate. Clinton was one of only two presidents to have ever been impeached – the other was Andrew Johnson in 1868. Neither was convicted or removed from office.

Mobocracy or Men of Reason?

How, though, should the president be chosen? Again, delegates worried about the passions of the people. If voters chose the president, they might be easily swayed. On the other hand, the delegates did want the people to have some voice.

The solution was to allow for a popular vote for president. The actual selection of a president, though, would be in the hands of a group of people, called electors, chosen by the state legislatures. The candidate getting the most of these electoral votes would win. By tradition, electors vote for the candidate who won their state's popular vote. In this way, the popular vote influences the electoral vote. Still, this is tradition, not the law. Electors are, in fact, free to vote for any candidate they wish.

The delegates assumed that the state legislatures would name serious, accomplished men as electors. They put their faith in 'men of reason' rather than the people.

57

Members of the League of Women Voters, 1920. The campaign for women's suffrage took more than 70 years to achieve success and required an amendment to the Constitution.

Fixed or Flexible?

The last question concerned the mechanism for making changes. The delegates had the experience of the Articles fresh in their minds. If they made it too difficult to change the Constitution, they would handicap future generations. If they made it too simple, the document would lose some of its power as a fundamental law.

The solution tried to achieve a balance. The delegates dropped the idea of unanimous consent from the states. As long as three-quarters of the states approved an amendment, it would become law. Only two-thirds of the members of both houses of Congress or two-thirds of the states were needed to offer changes for consideration.

Still, any person wanting to make a change would have to rally strong support for their idea. A simple majority was not enough. They needed two-thirds of the Congress and three-quarters of the states.

Heated Debate

In September of 1787, the delegates finished their work. They submitted the Constitution to the Congress for consideration. Opponents moved to reject it, but were defeated. Congress sent the document to the states for approval. Once nine states voted to ratify the Constitution, it would go into effect.

Alexander Hamilton (1775–1804), one of the authors of the *Federalist Papers*, believed in the establishment of a strong federal government. He went on to serve in Washington's Cabinet as secretary of the treasury.

The issues that the delegates had argued over in the Convention were raised again – and foes of the new plan raised another. The Constitution had no guarantees of individual rights. These had been the cornerstone of the British Constitution. Some critics said they would never accept the Constitution without such guarantees.

Leaders on both sides wrote essays for or against ratification. Most famous are the essays called the *Federalist Papers* (supporters of the Constitution had taken the name 'Federalists'). Alexander Hamilton wrote most of them, but Madison and Jay contributed as well. In these essays, published anonymously, they pointed out the weaknesses of the Articles and explained the benefits of the Constitution. They answered critics and reassured the wavering.

Becoming a Reality

Delaware quickly approved the Constitution and Pennsylvania followed soon after. By early June, nine states – the number required for the Constitution to take effect – had done so. Still, all eyes were on Virginia and New York. If these large states did not agree to join the new government, its success would be in danger.

The debate in Virginia raged for more than three weeks. As had been the case in Massachusetts, the issue of personal rights was a major stumbling block. As in Massachusetts, the state approved the document while insisting on the addition of amendments that guaranteed those rights. New York followed in July. The Convention there approved the Constitution, but only by three votes. It, too, insisted on a Bill of Rights. The old Congress prepared to make way for the new government.

Among the first orders of business of the new Congress was to pass the Bill of Rights. The first ten amendments to the Constitution guaranteed such basic rights as freedom of speech, assembly and religion. They ensured that citizens would have fair trials and would not be subject to illegal searches.

Solon's reform of the laws of Athens in 593BC allowed citizens of all classes to participate in the assembly and public law courts. The Convention rejected such a step towards direct democracy.

The Framers and the People

In ancient Athens, all citizens took part in the city's assembly. The same is true of New England town meetings, both in the 1700s and today. These were direct democracies. That is, all the people, or all the voters, had a direct voice in government decisions.

The framers of the Constitution did not want a direct democracy. One reason was practicality. They thought that a direct democracy was appropriate only for a small area. In a country as large as the United States, it would be impossible to bring all citizens together to make decisions. They were creating a republic.

The second reason reflected principle. They did not want direct democracy because they did not trust the people. They worried that the people were too passionate – that the people could be persuaded by a

ROGER SHERMAN.

Roger Sherman (1721–93) was the only man to sign all four great documents of the Revolution – the Articles of Association (1774), the Declaration of Independence (1776), the Articles of Confederation (1777) and the Constitution of the United States (1787).

demagogue instead of being guided by reason. As Roger Sherman of Connecticut said:

 [The people] should have as little to do as may be about the Government. They [lack] information and are liable to be misled.

The people, they believed, could easily be swayed. A clever politician could stir up their passions to gain power. One reason that Madison admired the Constitution was that it prevented the 'tyranny of the majority'. The massacre of tens of thousands of Armenians by the Turks, the killing of millions of Jews by the Nazis, and the persecution of millions of African Americans by whites in the American South show how right Madison was to fear that power.

Fear of the People

Fear of the people shaped several aspects of the Constitution. Election of the president by electors and not the popular vote is one example. The Senate is another. The framers saw it as a collection of wise leaders who could serve as a brake when a president or the House acted hastily or unwisely. Senators were not elected but chosen by state legislatures. Not until the early 1900s were they elected directly by the people.

Nevertheless, the framers accepted the Enlightenment idea that the people's consent was needed for government to be legitimate. Electing leaders was the tradition to which they were accustomed. It was the principle of government they believed in. As Madison wrote:

It is evident that no other form [than a republic] would be reconcilable with the genius of the people of America; with the fundamental principles of the Revolution; or with that honourable determination … to rest all our political experiments on the capacity of mankind for self-government.

THE AMERICAN EXPERIENCE

The New Republic

On 30 April 1789, George Washington took the oath of office as president. John Adams was the first vice president; Jefferson, Edmund Randolph and Hamilton headed executive departments. The Senate included Richard Henry Lee and Ellsworth. Sherman, Gerry and Madison sat in the House. Jay was the first Chief Justice of the Supreme Court. The decisions, actions and words of this generation shaped the American future.

A crowd acclaims Washington as he comes to New York to be inaugurated. Without cash at the time, Washington had to borrow money to make the trip.

Washington Sets the Course

Washington set important precedents for the presidency. He took the simple title 'Mr President' to avoid creating any sense of a monarchy. He appointed people to head up the executive departments, creating the first presidential Cabinet. He hardly ever used his vice president, a practice that has only been reversed very recently. Also, Washington served only two terms. No president ran for a third term until 1940. Later, an amendment made two terms a firm limit.

At one point, Washington brought the draft of a treaty to the Senate to discuss. When the senators debated it down to the smallest detail, he vowed never to do so again. Ever since, presidents have negotiated treaties and then submitted them for approval. Also, during his presidency, Congress passed a law making it clear that the Senate did not have to approve the president's removal of someone from office.

Judicial Review

One of the Supreme Court's early decisions established an important precedent. In 1801, John Marshall was named Chief Justice of the Supreme Court. Two years

John Marshall (1755–1835) – though a Virginian like Jefferson and Madison – favoured a strong central government, along with Adams and Hamilton.

Do modern American political conventions reflect the values of the Revolutionary generation?

later, he wrote the decision *Marbury* v. *Madison*. In it, Marshall stated that the Supreme Court has the power to overturn any law that goes against the Constitution. This power of judicial review is an important feature of the American system of government.

Party Politics and Orderly Transition

During Washington's term as president, two groups emerged. These groups had very different ideas on many issues that the nation faced. They eventually became the first American political parties. Adams, Hamilton and their followers were the Federalists. Jefferson, Madison and their allies were called Republicans. (This party later became the Democrats of today.) These two groups disagreed strongly.

Nevertheless, this generation set another important precedent – the peaceful transfer of power. In 1800, Thomas Jefferson defeated John Adams in a presidential election. Despite the bitter campaign, Adams stepped down and the Federalists accepted the new president.

By the 1840s, settlers were moving to the Pacific West. In the 1860s, railroads crossed the American continent.

Westward Expansion

The Revolutionary generation did not think the United States would be limited to the original thirteen states. But what status would new states have? These leaders could have given new states less power than the original ones. Doing so would have shattered the principles on which the Revolution was fought – the ideas of representation and self-government – but kept more power for their states.

They rejected this step. The Northwest Ordinance of 1787 set in law the idea that new states would have power equal to the original ones. This decision made the expansion of the United States possible. If new states did not enjoy this equality, people living in territories would have been reluctant to join the United States.

The Issue of Slavery

The Revolutionary generation had kept slavery alive. Over the next decades, the market for cotton boomed in the South and, as a result, slavery became even more important. The Southern states became even more deeply committed to protecting slavery, and to spreading it further. At the same time, Northern states opposed this expansion. This tension dominated American politics from 1820 to 1860.

Nearly 200,000 African Americans fought in the Union army during the Civil War.

It took a violent and bloody civil war to end slavery. New amendments to the Constitution outlawed slavery, declared that the rights of a citizen could not be denied because of race, and guaranteed African Americans the right to vote.

Equal Protection

Though slavery had ended, African Americans still suffered. Another 100 years were needed to put those ideas into action. The civil rights movement of the 1950s and 1960s pushed the government to end legal discrimination against African Americans.

In striking down discriminatory laws, some say that the federal government finally redeemed the promise of the Declaration that all people have the rights to 'life, liberty, and the pursuit of happiness'. Others argue that the injustice and prejudice still faced by African Americans proves this idea empty. The economic position of African Americans still lags behind that of white Americans – a legacy of the cancer of slavery.

'Remember the Ladies'

While he was away at the Continental Congress, John Adams carried on a lively correspondence with his wife Abigail. In one of her letters, she cautioned him to,

> *Remember the Ladies ... Do not put such unlimited power into the hands of the husbands. Remember all men would be tyrants if they could.*

Despite the fact that many women helped win the Revolution, women gained little from independence or the Constitution. In 1848, a group of women and men demanded women's rights in familiar words:

> *We hold these truths to be self-evident: that all men and women are created equal.*

Not until 1920 did women win the right to vote in national elections and not until the 1960s and 1970s did women have guarantees of personal rights. Even then, an amendment to the Constitution that would explicitly guarantee equal rights to women failed to achieve ratification in the 1970s. Many women felt that they remained as second-class citizens.

Martin Luther King, Jr. leading demonstrators to the state capitol in Montgomery, Alabama at the end of a five-day march. King was a leading figure in the civil rights movement of the 1950s and 1960s.

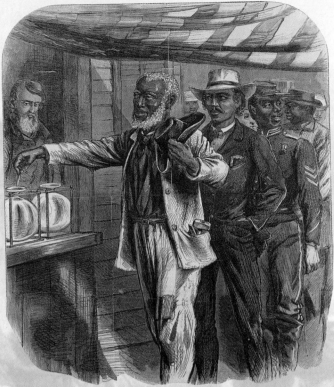

This image, from an 1867 magazine, depicts African Americans queuing up to vote for the first time.

Voting Rights

At first, only a fraction of Americans could vote. Over time, that changed. In the 1820s, most states dropped property ownership as a requirement for that right. This step still limited voting to white men only.

In 1870, the Fifteenth Amendment gave African American men the right to vote. They voted in large numbers at first, but soon white governments in the South limited their rights. Not until the 1960s did the federal government overturn those laws with the Voting Rights Act of 1965. In 1920, women, half the population, finally won the right to vote. Four years later, so did the Native Americans. In 1971, the right was extended to eighteen-year-olds.

These changes give almost all Americans the basic right that the Revolutionary generation wanted – the right to choose the leaders who would make the laws that affected them.

Was it a Revolution?

Why, then, is this event called the American Revolution? Did it bring about revolutionary changes in America? Suppose you visited the American colonies in 1775 and went back to see the states in 1789. The social order would seem the same. Wealthy landowners and merchants still dominated society and politics. Labourers and common farmers could vote only if they owned property. Particular churches were established, or given official recognition by the government in many states, just as they had been before the war.

Other groups in society still had low status, as before. Women generally had no political power. Hundreds of thousands of blacks were still held in slavery. Native Americans were even worse off than before the war. After all, the British had been willing to prevent the colonists from moving onto Indian lands.

Why did Native Americans back the British during the Revolution? Did they benefit in any way?

Except for Loyalists, the wealthy, landed families of colonial times kept their wealth and their land.

Social Changes

On the other hand, society had changed, and the ideas of the Revolution spurred those changes. By 1790, most of the new states had passed new laws about the inheritance of land. Instead of being passed intact to the oldest son, land had to be divided among all the children. This movement grew out of the Revolutionary ideology. Women did make some gains. In all but two states, the new laws of inheritance gave daughters the right to inherit land. New Jersey, alone among the new states, even gave women the right to vote (though that right was taken away in 1807). As we saw earlier, the idea of equality had persuaded some states to end slavery.

While several states kept their established churches, the idea of religious freedom had gained appeal. Indeed, the First Amendment to the Constitution, ratified in 1791, guaranteed freedom of worship.

The Revolution, then, did bring about some social changes. But the real difference from 1776 to 1789 was political. The Revolution had taken political power out of the hands of Britain's King and Parliament. It had firmly placed that power in the hands of ordinary people, albeit a very small group of white males who owned property. Still, this was a revolution. Around the world, countries were led by emperors, kings and princes. In the United States, the leader was not addressed as 'Your Highness' or 'Your Excellency'. He was simply 'Mr President'.

The American Revolution was a watershed in world history. It was the first war of national liberation. For the first time, a colony had won independence from its parent country. It would not be the last.

THE WORLD STAGE

Great Britain

Arguments over American representation in Parliament affected British politics. In the 1700s, many areas of Britain were no more directly represented in Parliament than the American colonies were. Representation, based on old rules, did not take into account shifts in the British population. Reforms did not come until 1832, but the debate began in the 1760s.

The British Empire

The Revolution had a profound impact on the Empire. Having lost the United States, the British were determined to hold onto Canada. In fact, as many as 40,000 Loyalists who fled the United States settled in Canada, where they were given land by the British. What had once been a French colony now had British settlements. Ironically, the English-speaking settlers wanted the rights they had enjoyed in the thirteen colonies. They forced the British to divide Canada into French-speaking and English-speaking provinces.

Thousands of Loyalists were settled by the British in Canada.

British control of another colonial area weakened when the British took troops out of Ireland to send them to North America. Later, the Irish were able to win more power for their own Parliament. This gain evaporated in 1800. But throughout the 1800s, Catholics in Ireland who fought for independence used the success of the American effort as a sign of hope.

The loss of the American colonies shifted the focus of the British Empire. Its holdings in India became more important, and became a new source of rivalry with France. Finally, this loss led the British to send convicts, who they had previously shipped to Georgia, to settle Australia.

Revolution in France

The American Revolution had two effects on France. Both contributed to the French Revolution. One was economic. France had a hefty two billion francs debt from the Seven Years War. French aid to the United States during the Revolution doubled that debt. This huge debt brought on a financial crisis in France that led directly to the French Revolution.

The other effect was ideological. The French became captivated by news and ideas from the United States. Growing numbers of books and pamphlets about the new country and its struggle were published in France. The new constitutions of the American states were also published, and were studied closely.

The key statement of the ideals of the French Revolution is similar to Jefferson's words in the Declaration of Independence:

Men are born and remain free and equal in rights.

This does not mean that the American Revolution caused the French Revolution. The ideas in Jefferson's Declaration were part of Enlightenment thinking, which was also widespread in France. Still, there was some influence flowing from the American success in creating a republican form of government.

In this allegory from the French Revolution, Liberty (right) and Justice (left) support the nation.

69

Spain and Spanish America

Spain, too, was hurt by the debt it took on in helping the Americans fight for independence. Several costly campaigns against the British weakened the Spanish government.

When the United States achieved independence, Spain began to worry. Its colonies in the Americas could try to do the same. The government tried to improve its control over those colonies. Meanwhile, people in those colonies pointed to the American Revolution as an example to follow. One pro-independence thinker wrote that there were two revolutionary examples to follow – the American and the French. He added:

Let us imitate ... the former; let us avoid with utmost care the fatal effects of the latter.

In the early 1800s, almost all of those colonies won their independence.

Inspiring Ideals

The American Revolution had some impact in other European countries at the time. The American struggle helped inspire democrats in the Netherlands who were struggling against aristocratic power in the 1780s and 1790s. Around this time, the constitution written by rebels in Belgium was influenced by the Articles of Confederation.

The Declaration of Independence has influenced others in this century. In 1945, Ho Chi Minh declared the independence of Vietnam from the French. He began his declaration by restating Jefferson's self-evident truths. Ironically, he later had to lead his country in a devastating war against the United States.

'Give Me Your Tired'

The independent United States influenced the world in other ways. One was as a magnet for immigration. Starting in the 1820s, hundreds of thousands of people came to the United States every decade for about 100 years. The influx slowed from the mid-1920s to 1950, when it began to rise again. By the late 1900s, nearly one million people were coming to America each year.

From 1880–1914, more than 25 million immigrants went to the United States. An 1883 poem inscribed on the Statue of Liberty extends a welcome: 'Give me your tired, your poor, your huddled masses yearning to breathe free....'

What factors does the cartoonist identify that drew immigrants to the United States?

Why did so many people go to the United States? Disasters, wars and political turmoil pushed many to leave their homes. Political and religious freedom drew others. Roger Daniels, a noted historian of American immigration, says another factor was most important:

 Most immigrants were not the poorest persons in the countries from which they came and ... economic betterment was the major motivating force.

Diversity

These immigrants have enriched the country's culture. Writers, painters and musicians have expressed the vision of countries as diverse as Italy, Cuba and China. That richness is born of growing diversity. Over time, the areas providing immigrants has changed. From 1820 to the 1920s, nearly 90 per cent of all immigrants came from Europe. Since the 1940s, nearly 40 per cent have come from Latin America. Europe and Asia provide about 30 per cent each.

As a result, the country is more diverse now than it ever was before. In 1790, about twenty per cent of the population was African American. The rest were almost all white Europeans, and almost all British. By the 1990s, whites were less than three-quarters of the population. African Americans were twelve per cent. Latinos formed ten per cent. Asian Americans were three per cent. Latinos are likely to become the largest minority group in the next century.

Leabharlanna Dhún Laoghaire · Ráth An Dúin

The United States in the World

This immigration has had an economic impact, too. Immigrant workers farmed land; built railroads, bridges and highways; made steel, cars and televisions. They provided the muscle that powered great economic growth. In the 1900s, the US economy became the largest in the world. Immigrants also supplied much of the scientific and technological expertise behind the economic growth.

The country's economic position and military might have made it an extremely powerful nation. By the close of the twentieth century, many were hailing the United States as the world's only 'superpower'. However, that power sometimes conflicts with ideals born in the Revolution. American leaders often say that the country stands for democracy and freedom, yet they have supported dictators who give their own people no freedom. The decades-long Cold War made American leaders turn a blind eye to the excesses of harsh rulers as long as they were not communists. A vocal minority in the United States protested at these choices. Many around the world joined in.

Even when the Cold War ended, American leaders were willing to deal with dictators in other countries, as long as they needed their friendship. Ironically, communist China provided the clearest example. By the 1990s, the communist rulers there were no longer shunned by the Americans, but actively courted. Trade between the two countries boomed. But whenever the Chinese cracked down on dissenters, abusing human rights, American leaders made only mild protests.

American leaders have also not hesitated to use their power to send troops to other countries when they have disliked a change in government. Several times in the 1900s, American troops landed in countries of the Caribbean or Central America to overthrow the results of a local revolution. Sometimes, those interventions were aimed at restoring governments that were friendly with American businesses. Sometimes, they aimed at defeating a communist movement. Whatever the cause, the actions were a show of force that was not always based on ideals. In economic terms, too, the United States has often acted to enhance its power, not to advance the ideas of the Declaration.

The Statue of Liberty, a gift from France, was meant to honour the centennial of American independence. It has come to be seen as a symbol of American ideals.

GLOSSARY

amendment a change to a law

Cabinet the heads of each executive department, who also serve as advisors to the president

charter an official document from the British government that granted an individual or group the right to start and maintain a colony

committees of correspondence groups formed in different towns so that rebellious colonists could communicate with one another

compromise an agreement in which each side gives up something it wants in order to reach a deal

desertion leaving an army before the time of service is done

duty a tax placed on an imported good

Enlightenment an intellectual movement of the 1700s which emphasised the importance of reason, insisted that all people enjoyed certain basic rights and that governments were formed for the benefit of the people

established describing a Church that is made the official religion by a government

foreclosure court action in which a person loses property because of a failure to pay the mortgage on it

House of Burgesses colonial assembly of Virginia

legislature part of the government that makes laws

Loyalists American colonists who remained loyal to Britain

martial law emergency government by the military

mercantilism an economic theory which held that a nation can increase its wealth through trade and by having colonies

mercenaries soldiers of one country who are paid to fight for another

militia a military force made of volunteers who serve part time

non-importation agreement plan in which people or businesses agree not to buy goods from another country

Parliament the legislature in Great Britain

precedent an action or decision that creates a tradition or customary practice that later actions or decisions can be based on

ratification formal approval of a proposal

repeal to pass a law making an earlier law invalid

siege surrounding a town or fort in hope of forcing the defenders to surrender

surveying using instruments to measure a tract of land before it is divided into lots and sold

veto an executive's power to make a law passed by the legislature invalid

TIMELINE OF EVENTS

1754		Seven Years War begins
1763	Feb:	Treaty of Paris ends Seven Years War
	May:	Pontiac's Rebellion begins
	Oct:	Proclamation of 1763 issued
1764		Parliament passes Sugar Act; colonists protest
1765	Mar:	Parliament passes Stamp Act
	May:	Virginia Resolves approved
	Oct:	Stamp Act Congress meets
1766		Stamp Act repealed; Declaratory Act passed
1767		Townshend Acts passed; colonists protest
1768	Feb:	Massachusetts Circular Letter
	Jul:	Massachusetts General Assembly dissolved
1769		Non-importation movement sweeps colonies
1770	Mar:	Boston Massacre
	Apr:	Most Townshend Acts repealed
1773	May:	Parliament passes Tea Act
	Dec:	Boston Tea Party
1774	Mar:	Parliament begins passing Coercive Acts (called 'Intolerable Acts' in colonies)
	May:	Gage arrives in Boston
	Sep:	First Continental Congress opens
1775	Feb – Mar:	Parliament passes laws that punish rebels and offer conciliation
	Apr:	Lexington and Concord
	May:	Second Continental Congress begins
	Jun:	Bunker Hill
	Jul:	Olive Branch Petition
	Aug:	George III declares colonies in rebellion
1776	Jan:	*Common Sense* published
	Mar:	British evacuate Boston
	May:	French agree to give aid to Americans
	Jul:	Congress declares independence
	Aug:	British win at Long Island
	Oct:	British win at Lake Champlain and White Plains
	Dec:	Americans win at Trenton
1777	Jan:	Americans win at Princeton
	Aug:	Americans win at Bennington
	Sep:	British win at Brandywine; Congress leaves Philadelphia
	Oct:	British win at Germantown; Americans win at Saratoga
	Dec:	France recognises United States
1778	Jun:	Congress rejects British peace plan; Battle of Monmouth
	Jul:	France declares war on Britain

Dec: British capture Savannah

1779 Jun: Spain declares war on Britain

Oct: American attempt to retake Savannah fails

1780 May: British capture Charleston

Aug: British win at Camden

Oct: Americans win at Kings Mountain

1781 Jan: Americans win at Cowpens

Feb: Robert Morris takes over finances

Mar: Articles of Confederation approved

Oct: Cornwallis surrenders at Yorktown

1782 Mar: Parliament votes to begin peace negotiations

Nov: Preliminary peace treaty signed

1783 Treaty of Paris signed

1784 Spain closes Mississippi River to Americans

1785 Congress passes Land Ordinance

1786 Feb: British refuse to leave forts in Great Lakes

July–Aug: American economy slows

Sep: Delegates meet in Annapolis Convention; Shays' Rebellion begins

1787 Feb: Shays' Rebellion defeated

May–Sep: Constitutional Convention

Jul: Congress passes Northwest Ordinance

Dec: Delaware is first state to ratify Constitution

1788 Jun: Ninth state ratifies Constitution, making it official; ratification in Virginia follows

Jul: New York ratifies Constitution

Nov: Last meeting of Congress under the Articles

1789 1 Apr: First Congress under Constitution meets

30 Apr: Washington sworn in as first president

FURTHER INFORMATION

There are many excellent books on the American Revolution. The following are especially useful.

John R. Alden, *A History of the American Revolution*, Da Capo Press, Cambridge, Mass., 1989

Colin Bonwick, *The American Revolution*, Macmillan, London, 1991

Don Cook, *The Long Fuse: How England Lost the American Colonies*, The Atlantic Monthly Press, New York, 1995

Edward Countryman, *The People's American Revolution*, British Association for American Studies, 1983

Theodore Draper, *A Struggle for Power: The American Revolution*, Abacus, London, 1997

M. J. Heale, *The American Revolution*, Methuen, London, 1986

Christopher Hibbert, *Redcoats and Rebels: The War for America 1770–1781*, Penguin, London, 1990

Pauline Maier, *American Scripture: Making the Declaration of Independence*, Pimlico, London, 2001

Robert Middlekauff, *The Glorious Cause*, Oxford University Press, Oxford, 1982

Christopher Moore, *The Loyalists: Revolution, Exile, Settlement*, McClelland & Stewart, Toronto, 1994

John Rhodehamel, ed., *The American Revolution: Writings from the War of Independence*, Library of America, New York, 2001

P. D. G. Thomas, *Revolution in America: Britain and the Colonies, 1763–1776*, University of Wales Press, Cardiff, 1992

The following websites contain interesting and reliable information on the American Revolution:
www.fordham.edu/halsall/mod/modsbook12.html
www.historyplace.com/text–index.html
www.pbs.org/ktca/liberty/
www.si.umich.edu/spies/

INDEX

Page numbers in *italics* indicate pictures.